WHEN SOMEONE YOU
LOVE DIES

WHEN SOMEONE YOU LOVE DIES

WILLIAM L. COLEMAN

Augsburg
MINNEAPOLIS

WHEN SOMEONE YOU LOVE DIES

Cover design: Lecy Design

Library of Congress Cataloging-in-Publication Data

Coleman, William L.
    When someone you love dies / William L. Coleman.
      p.   cm.
    Includes bibliographical references.
    ISBN (invalid) 0-8006-2670-4 (alk. paper) :
    1. Death—Religious aspects—Christianity—Juvenile literature.
I. Title.
BT825.H645   1994
344.73'078—dc20
[347.30478]   94-2953
                                       CIP
                                       AC

Manufactured in the U.S.A.   AF 9-2670

98   97   96   4   5   6   7   8   9   10

Contents

Acknowledgments

Thanks for the help.

I want to thank the many people who have helped make this book possible. Both professionals and families have contributed a great deal toward our understanding of death and children. Hopefully this book will serve to free young people from the unreasonable burden of death and make life a richer experience for each of them.

Suggestions for Adults

Smart people don't try to cover up death. If you attempt to shield children from death, you could do them a great deal of harm. Follow your better instincts and let children know exactly what's going on when death touches the people they care about.

If you spend ten minutes a day with a child for two weeks, that child's life could be changed. By simply explaining four or five facts about death, you could spare that child decades of confusion and pain.

Unfortunately many people still believe that the less a child knows the better. You should rise above that nonsense and help a child by communicating in an open fashion.

At a very early age children know something about death. Almost as soon as they realize that squirrels, plants, and cats are alive, they are equally aware that they die. Since they will find out early, the most helpful thing you can do is to make sure they understand correctly.

I haven't met you, but I admire you. By spending time with a child, you are doing the work of God. Feel fulfilled and worthwhile because you are willing to touch a life in a positive and healing way.

As you use this volume, I would like to suggest a few guidelines to make the experience even more valuable.

1. *Don't be in a hurry.* The book is designed for a slow, steady pace. Be patient. Read only a few pages at a time. If the children want to stop and ask something else, be willing to go in that direction. Let them know you are available to help and you aren't merely trying to get through a book.

2. *Be positive.* There is a lot that's negative about death, so don't be afraid to mention the benefits. Heaven, hope, relief, and reunion are each valid subjects.

Also admit the downside. Separation is real and painful, as children already know.

3. *Never, never lie to children.* If you wreck a child's trust, you have caused a serious injury. In our desire to protect, we often tend to cover up and exaggerate.

Children need the facts as well as the feelings.

4. *Be a good listener.* Listening is at the heart of communication. We don't know how a child feels and there is only one way to find out: We have to hear him out.

Let children use their own words. Try not to correct them. When children speak of heaven and hope, be as accepting as possible.

5. *Accept children's feelings.* However children describe their feelings is fine. If they refer to hate, love, being sad, glad, relieved, or whatever, don't argue with their feelings. Try to hear what they are saying and be happy that they could get it out.

6. *Encourage any questions.* Don't be surprised if a child wants to know about AIDS or cancer or whatever. Be prepared for gory questions about accidents or body damage. Stay cool and direct. Try not to be shocked.

7. *Show your feelings.* Don't pretend to be sad, but don't hide your sadness either. Your honest emotions will give the child permission to show his or her feelings, too.

When we hide facts or feelings, we teach deception.

Time is a healing element, but time alone makes lousy medicine. Time, love, and information are the perfect mix.

There are three areas that need special attention when discussing death with children:

1. *Facts*. Explain what actually happened to cause the death and what will now happen to the body.

2. *Feelings*. Get past the question of how we "should" feel and allow the child to express how he "does" feel.

3. *Faith*. If you don't bring up the questions of heaven, hope, and the hereafter, children probably will. Help them express their faith as well as their doubts.

Too many of us look at death as the perfect opportunity to teach. It would be better to go light on the teaching aspect and concentrate on feelings. Grieve, hurt, heal, hope, be glad, and agonize with the child.

The Mystery of Death

When I was a child, my baby sister died. I remember all the hushed tones and the little storefront funeral home around the corner from our house.

What I don't recall is anyone ever discussing her death. Our parents were caught up in their own grief, which I'm sure was intense. But I don't remember anyone sitting down with me and explaining what was going on.

That's the way it was. Today many adults are more willing to talk to children. Adults also take more time to listen.

Be glad that you have someone to talk to. Ask that person every question you can think of. Describe your feelings about each part of death and funerals. Don't be shy.

Understand everything you can about the mystery of death. Death is an important part of life.

Bill Coleman

All of Us Are Changing

Did you make a hand mold when you were in kindergarten? To make a hand mold the teacher pours plaster into a dish and has the student stick his hand on it. When the mold hardens, there is a print of the child's fingers and palm.

A few years later, the student who puts a hand on top of that print can see how much he or she has changed. Every year we change a little. Some years we change a lot.

Life is change. We get bigger, stronger, taller, faster, and grow more hair. As we get old, we often become slower, weaker, shorter, and lose some of our hair.

We keep changing until someday we die. Death is part of our change. It's normal. It happens to all of us. Our bodies won't work forever.

Most of us change slowly. It may take seventy or eighty years for our bodies to die. Some people get very sick or their bodies wear out early or they may die in an accident. Those are the exceptions. Our bodies are made to last a long time.

If we look at a picture of our grand-parents ten years ago and look at them now, we can see the change. Their hair is probably white today, but it wasn't always white. Their skin may show some wrinkles. They may have less hair.

It's easy to see the change in old people and in children. Parents change, too, but more slowly. Sometimes parents put on weight or get "potbellies" or take more naps than they used to.

All of us need to talk about death because death is natural. We talk about food or the weather or mountains because that is normal. Some day a person we know or care about is going to die. It could be a relative or a friend. If we don't talk about it first, we may be terribly confused when it happens.

Death doesn't have to be a gory, scary, creepy subject. Our bodies change, and eventually we die. If we understand that, we can accept death as part of life.

Why Did Grandpa Die?

If your parents' automobile stops running, there is always a reason. Maybe it ran out of gas, the starter broke, the alternator wouldn't turn over, or something else quit working. Sometimes a car won't run for two or three reasons. The battery is low, the distributor cap is cracked, or whatever.

There isn't anything magic or mysterious about a car not running. Even if the mechanic can't find the problem, there is certainly a mechanical cause for the breakdown.

In the same way, people do not die mysteriously or magically. When a person dies, either one part of him or a number of his parts stop working.

If our lungs stop working, we can no longer process air, and our bodies will die. When our heart breaks down, it no longer pumps, and life will be over. If we get cancer, certain parts of our bodies are destroyed, and our body-machine eventually won't operate.

What stops our bodies from working? Diseases, old age, poisons, and accidents are the main reasons. Gunshot wounds, stabs, and AIDS, can also shut us down forever.

Too often we talk about death in hushed tones, and everything sounds spooky. Some people act like cemeteries are filled with ghosts and everything is eerie and scary. As sad as death is, the facts are that a body has stopped working. None of us can go on living if certain parts of our bodies break down.

The two most common causes of death today are heart attacks and cancer. We can suffer from either one and still live, but if they are bad enough, we will die.

The Bible tells us that death is normal. Sooner or later our bodies will stop functioning. God says there is "a time to be born and a time to die" (Ecclesiastes 3:2).

If your grandfather has died, do you know why his body stopped working? Would you like to know? If you would, then you need to ask someone who knows the facts. Don't ask someone for an opinion or a guess. Ask an adult who has reason to know exactly what happened.

When we are curious about something, it's like having a large blank spot in our memory. If that blank spot bothers us, for whatever reason, we should try and get it filled in.

Tell an adult you would like to know why your grandfather died. Most adults would be glad to give the answer.

Going to a Funeral

When I was in grade school, a friend of mine was killed when sand at a construction site caved in on him. He and two others were exploring when the accident happened. The newspapers said my friend tried to drag one of his companions through the sand to the top, but he couldn't make it.

I clearly remember going to the funeral home to see my friend's body laid out in a casket. He looked too young to be dead. There were flowers all around on stands, and his parents were crying.

Funerals aren't fun, but they are interesting. Children don't usually go to many funerals, but when they do, they can ask a lot of questions. Sometimes they want to see where the dead person's feet are. That's because the casket lid is split in half and usually only the head and shoulders can be seen.

When they think no one is looking, some children put their fingers under the dead person's nose to see if that person is breathing. Sometimes children wonder what it is like in the back rooms where the bodies are kept.

Funeral homes (also called mortuaries) are normally solemn places where people come to "pay their respects" to the family and to say good-bye. The dead person can't tell who is there, but the visit is thoughtful anyway.

In some cases there is no body for people to see. A family might choose to have the body buried the same day the person dies. Or the family might wish to cremate (burn up) the body before the funeral.

There are many different customs at funerals. Some people cry a great deal. Others don't. Some families are loud and noisy. Others whisper and are quiet. Some funeral services have music and singing. Others have a minister or some other person say some words about the dead person.

How do you feel about going to funerals? You should not be forced to attend if you don't want to go. But many good things can come from being at a funeral.

If you want to, you can have one last look at the dead person's body. You can get together with other people who also loved the dead person. You can pray and think about God and hear words that might be encouraging to everyone. You can listen to music that may make you feel better.

Funerals aren't trips to haunted houses. Usually they are times of love and pleasant memories. They are also occasions for hope as we remember how Jesus Christ has overcome death for each of us.

You shouldn't feel forced to go, but you might find help by attending a funeral.

What Is Heaven Like?

Those of us who are Christians believe in heaven. When we die, we go to heaven. But what is heaven really like? Do we float on clouds or listen to harp music all day? Will there be skiing in heaven?

The Bible doesn't tell us many facts about the place, so it's hard to imagine. Let's put our minds to work and try to pretend what heaven must be like. Take each category and fill it in exactly as you would like it to be.

1. *Music.*

Will there be singing in heaven? Will there be choirs or duets or quartets? What kind of music—classical, rock, country? You decide. Make up the instruments and groups.

2. *Transportation*

How will people get around? Do you picture chariots, wings, jet-propelled clouds, pogo sticks or what? Do people fly, walk, run, jog, or simply put their hands on their heads and they are there?

3. *Food.*

Will we need food at all? Will there be pizza in heaven? What about Sloppy Joes or soft drinks? (Don't anyone dare suggest angel food cake.) Will there be french fries? Make up your own menu.

4. *Worship.*

Will we worship God by sitting still with our heads bowed, or will we jump and shout? Are there special jobs that God will have us busily doing?

5. *People.*

Will we recognize each other in heaven? Can we look for a favorite uncle, aunt, or grandparent? Will we see a brother or sister who died before we did?

There is no harm in guessing what heaven will be like. Heaven may be even better than we can create in our minds. Whatever it's like, some of our relatives already know more about it than we do. They have been there for a week or two or maybe for years.

Christians don't believe we just stop breathing and walk out into darkness. Death is a trip to a better place. Until we get there we might as well enjoy ourselves by thinking about how it will be good.

"But in keeping with his promise we are looking forward to a new heaven and a new earth, the home of righteousness" (2 Peter 3:13).

How Do We Get Home?

It was late at night when Jill's family began the trip home. Her parents sat in the front seat while she sprawled out in the back. As the car hummed down the highway, Jill found a seat cushion, lay back in the corner, and soon fell into a deep sleep.

When she woke up, sunlight was hitting her in the eyes. "Where am I?" she wondered. Rubbing her eyes, Jill began to recognize her surroundings. The bed, the covers, her favorite dolls. She was at home in her own bedroom.

Now she knew exactly what had happened. She had gone to sleep in the car on the ride home. When they all arrived home, one of her parents picked her up and carried her inside and placed Jill in her own bed.

Jill hadn't felt anything. She didn't remember anything. But she had been carried gently, quietly, safely from one place to the other without realizing it.

Death must be much like Jill's trip. Once she went to sleep, she had no fear.

Everything was taken care of. The people who loved her picked her up and carried her home.

One of the ways the Bible describes death is "sleep." Death must be pleasant and peaceful. Those who have "gone to sleep" are now with Jesus Christ (1 Thessalonians 4:13-14.)

Hard to Talk About

"Your grandmother died last night of a heart attack," Jenny's mother told her at the breakfast table. "The funeral will be Tuesday afternoon."

That was all Jenny's mother said about Grandmother's death. Later they discussed what to wear, who was coming to the funeral, and how Jenny would make up her schoolwork. They talked about what needed to be done, but they never shared how they felt.

Many parents and other adults feel awkward trying to discuss death and emotions. When they were children and someone died, probably no one talked to them. They grew up thinking death was "spooky" or "too depressing," so today they aren't comfortable with the subject.

Adults tell themselves, "I don't want to tell my children about death. They can't handle that." But what adults really mean is, "I don't want to tell my children about death. *I* can't handle it."

Be patient with parents. Help them open up and share their feelings. There are two good ways to get a discussion going with adults.

1. *Tell them you want to know how this person died.* When the adult begins talking, ask more questions, like Was she sick long? Did it hurt? or whatever.

2. *Tell them it's all right to discuss death.* Explain that you can handle it and you want to understand what is going on.

This is called "giving permission." You are saying, "It's OK to talk to me about death. I can handle it."

When you talk with an adult about death, the conversation might become sad. Both of you might cry. But that's all right.

Not all of our conversations are happy, silly, or cheerful. Death is a serious situation. Someone who used to be part of our life is no longer a part of our life. We may miss that person terribly. If we feel sad and want to talk about that sadness, then we should.

Adults need to talk about death as much as children do. We can help each other if we agree to discuss death.

A father said to his son, "Your grandfather died this morning. Go ahead and cry if you want, but after today don't ever mention it again."

Too bad that father couldn't handle the death of Grandfather. He and his son could have felt better about death if they had been free to discuss it.

Draw a Picture

Sometimes it's hard to say exactly how we feel. We might feel good and bad, happy and sad all about the same thing.

How do we feel if we used to have a cat but now the cat is gone? We might have great memories, and we might smile just thinking about that cat. At the same time we are sad because the cat isn't around anymore.

And sometimes we are confused. If the cat tore up our furniture and went to the bathroom on our bed, we may not miss the cat very much.

When someone dies, we might not be sure how we feel. If he was in a great deal of pain, we might be glad that his suffering is over.

If it's hard to say how we feel, it may be easier to draw a picture of what is going on inside us. But how do we draw feelings? One way is to draw the people involved in the feelings. Maybe the picture will include the person who has died or your family together without that person or a picture

29

of yourself looking sad. The drawing might have furniture or a special room or a special gift.

You are free to use your imagination. It's no help to simply draw a picture that you saw somewhere else.

There are no wrong feelings. Be honest about what is going on. There is no need to pretend you feel one way when the fact is you feel another way.

After you draw a picture, show it to an adult friend. Parents, teachers, counselors, or ministers might be good people to show it to. Grandparents, close neighbors, older brothers or sisters also might like to see it.

Spend a few minutes explaining the picture. Why did you draw it this way? You will know exactly why you drew certain parts that way. But there could be parts of the picture that are a mystery even to you.

Many of us find it much easier to deal with death if we put it on paper. It helps us see what has happened. We usually feel better after we express ourselves in some way.

We Have Regrets

Mary had told her grandmother she would be over to see her on Saturday. They had planned to go shopping at the mall and later have lunch together. Grandmother had called and set up the schedule as she had many times before. The two of them had plenty to talk about when they were together.

When Saturday rolled around, Mary's mother tried to wake her daughter up, but the twelve-year-old wouldn't budge. "I'll call Grandmother later," Mary mumbled as she snuggled back under the covers.

Mary didn't get up until noon. And she didn't call her grandmother. But she intended to call and apologize. She knew what she had done was wrong.

On Tuesday Grandmother had a heart attack and died. When Mary heard the news, she felt crushed. The grandmother she loved so much had died before Mary could say she was sorry.

When someone we love dies, we may feel guilty. We may have regrets. We may wish we had been kinder, wish we had spoken less harshly, wish we had listened or spent time with that person. That's part of loving people. We miss them and wish we had shared our love with them more.

Some of us have regrets because we know we did something wrong. Maybe we took money out of that person's wallet. Maybe we told a lie. We might have taken some clothing without asking and didn't give it back.

Most of us have some regrets. We can think of something we could have done better. Something we could have said but never got around to saying.

The person has now died. We can no longer correct those mistakes. We can't tell him anything because he can't hear us. We can't keep an appointment because he won't be there. If we stole from him, we can return whatever it was to the family (but that's unusual.)

We can't help anyone if we continue to let our heart break with regret. Everyone makes mistakes. None of us can change the past.

The best we can do now is to forgive ourselves as God forgives us. Forgiving ourselves can be hard to do, but it's the right thing. Then we need to concentrate on the good memories we have about the person who died. Remember the times we smiled together, laughed together, did things, went places.

Don't carry around regrets that you can't fix anyway. Focus on the happy times and enjoy the good memories.

Write a Letter

Was there something you wanted to say? Is there something you have thought of and you wish you could say now?

You know the person can't hear you, but still you want to get it off your mind or your heart. Have you thought about writing a letter to the person who has died?

It isn't a silly idea at all. Writing is a way of expressing ourselves. By putting something on paper, we let out the emotions we have stuffed inside.

Maybe you aren't comfortable putting your feelings on paper. There was a time when I didn't feel comfortable about it either.

In your letter let's say that spelling doesn't count and you can punctuate any way you want. I know a writer who doesn't use any capital letters when he writes. That's all right this time, too.

Letters can be long or short. Letters can be written in full sentences or in poetry. Sometimes poetry rhymes, but most of the time it doesn't. Letters can be written on fine stationery or on a brown paper bag. The meaning of a letter like this is more important than any of its parts.

If you write a letter to someone who has died, what will you say? The letter might:

> thank him or her.
>
> express your anger.
>
> apologize.
>
> tell the person that you miss him or her.
>
> mention the good times you had.
>
> say you love him or her.
>
> explain you will take care of the person's pet

Your letter will be different from anyone else's because it will describe how you feel. There could be plenty of other reasons besides the few examples on this list.

Make it your letter. Say it your way.

After you write the letter, the next question is where do you send it? The post office doesn't have delivery to heaven, and you can't FAX it on a space telephone. But there are ways to send the letter.

If there is still time, you might ask if you can put it in the coffin. Possibly it could

35

be read at the funeral. You could ask a relative to read it for you. That way you will know that someone has heard how you feel.

Another possibility is to place the letter in your dresser drawer and leave it for a while. After two weeks or a month, you can take it out and read it again. Then you can either put it back in the drawer or throw it away. Some people prefer to burn the letter.

Letters have a lot of possibilities. They are a great way to get things said that need to be said.

Who Will Take His Place?

When eleven-year-old Toby died in a car accident, his brother, Lance, tried to take his place. He volunteered to carry out the trash because that used to be Toby's job. Lance joined a basketball team because his brother had belonged to one. Maybe, Lance thought to himself, his parents could come and watch him play, and that would make them feel better about losing their other son.

Sometimes we try to take the place of someone who has died. We want to step in and be the person he used to be. We mean well, but we can't take the place of another person.

Belinda tried the same thing when her Aunt Terri died. Her uncle was so lonely that he practically gave up. Two months after his wife's funeral he was hardly eating at all, and his house was turning into a junk pile. Twelve-year-old Belinda decided she needed to make a move and take Aunt Terri's place.

A couple of times she helped fix meals and she straightened up the living room.

It was a pretty cool idea. But soon Belinda became overly burdened about her uncle's condition.

After another week of Belinda's coming over too often, her uncle sat down and had a frank talk with her. He expressed his appreciation for the work and told her she was the greatest niece in the world. Her help convinced him, he said, how important it was for him to stand on his own two feet and take charge of his life.

Belinda felt relieved because she was realizing that she couldn't be Aunt Terri.

You have to admire people who want to step in and help. Everyone needs help sometimes. It's too bad when someone goes too far and actually tries to take another person's place. It can't be done. The best gift we can give is to be ourselves.

Does It Hurt to Die?

I used to wonder that. When I was a child I can remember holding my breath and trying to imagine it. What if I didn't take another breath, I would ask myself. What would that feel like?

Since I have never died, that's a little hard to answer, but I'll try anyway. I have seen people die, and I have read the accounts of others who thought they almost died.

The people I saw die had a look of peace on their faces. They had become weak and tired and weren't afraid of death. Their breathing slowed. It finally quit, and they were gone.

A man who almost died gave death high marks. He said it was a pleasant experience, and he wasn't sure he wanted to come back.

Often there is pain associated with death. If someone is in an accident, she could hurt terribly before she dies. However, she could go into shock and feel little pain. Any number of awful diseases like cancer can cause miserable suffering.

But does it actually hurt to die? It doesn't appear to. Whatever makes us die might be painful, but the act of death itself may be very peaceful. Usually we think of death as something that ends our human suffering. That's probably true.

What causes us to die might hurt. However, the act of leaving this life to enter the next life doesn't seem to be painful.

A leading authority on death is Jesus Christ, the Son of God. He lived in a real body like the rest of us. Jesus suffered terribly on a cross and then died. The Bible tells us he returned from the dead after spending three days in the grave.

Since Jesus experienced death and came back to life, he knows a great deal about it. I trust him to someday guide me through death, so I will live forever with God.

I want to know about dying, but I realize that I can't learn everything. That's why it's important to trust Jesus Christ to lead me through the "valley of death."

"Christ died for our sins according to the Scriptures, that he was buried, that he was raised on the third day according to the Scriptures" 1 Corinthians 15:3-4.

Talking about Them

"When we get there, keep your feet off the couch," Mrs. Sonderson reminded her children. "Aunt Jean doesn't want shoes all over her nice furniture."

"And don't keep eating the mints," Mr. Sonderson added.

"Why does she put the mints in the dish," asked ten-year-old Nate, "if she doesn't want us to eat them?"

"Never you mind," said Mrs. Sonderson. "Don't go around begging for cookies either. If she wants you to have some, she will offer them. And if she does, only take one."

The family van sliced through the rain.

"Are we going to just sit still in the living room for hours like we usually do?" Laura wondered out loud.

"I'd think you would like this chance to visit your Aunt Jean." Mr. Sonderson adjusted the wiper switch to make the wipers move faster. "We don't get to see her that often."

"What in the world is there to talk about?" Nate asked.

"Oh, there are all sorts of things," Mrs. Sonderson contributed. "Ask her about her cats. She loves them. And ask about her feather collection. You know she lights up when you ask her about her trip to St. Louis."

"That was five years ago," Laura grumped.

"Talk to her about anything," Mr. Sonderson agreed, "but don't bring up Uncle Lenny. The funeral was too recent. Besides, it will probably make her cry."

Mrs. Sonderson nodded. "The funeral was just a month ago."

"What if she wants to talk about Uncle Lenny?" Nate asked.

"Then change the subject," Mr. Sonderson insisted. "There's no sense in being morbid."

"I liked Uncle Lenny," Laura said. "I thought he was funny."

"Don't say that to Aunt Jean," warned Mrs. Sonderson. "You don't want her falling apart while we're there."

"Can I ask her if I can see his old uniform?" Nate pushed the issue.

"Nathan, you do and I'll scream!" Mr. Sonderson's voice grew firm.

That's the way some families handle death. They make it a point to never mention the dead person.

People who know about grieving say that talking about the dead person helps us deal with our grief. We don't need to discuss him or her all the time, but some conversation can make us all feel better.

A Salad Bar of Emotions

Have you ever been to a restaurant that has a salad bar? It's a table with maybe a dozen different bowls of food. There are noodles, cole slaw, peas, pudding, fruit, and so it goes.

You can pick and choose and stack up your plate with your favorite foods. If you want, you can come back later and help yourself to more.

When a person close to us dies, our emotions are like a salad bar. We might be

sad	confused
mad	lonely
angry	relieved
indifferent	afraid
sick	sorry.

Or maybe none of these describes exactly how you feel. There could be another emotion that isn't on the list. It's a different bowl that you don't see on this table. And sometimes salad bars have two bowls of the same thing. Maybe you feel like you have two bowls of sorry or two bowls of angry.

Salad bars aren't the same every day. One day there are pickles and the next day there is watermelon. It's possible to feel confused one day, sad another, and relieved the third.

Another thing about salad bars is that the menu can change permanently. Suppose there used to be bowls of baked beans every day but now there are none. The baked-bean days are over. The same thing happens if you used to feel sick at night because of the death. Later the sickness stops, and that feeling does not show up on your salad bar of emotions anymore.

Let's look at this again. How are emotions like a salad bar?

1. There are lots of different emotions on the salad bar.

2. We might have two bowls or a double portion of some feelings.

3. Feelings might change from day to day.

4. Some emotions used to appear on the salad bar, but they don't show up anymore.

How would you describe your salad bar of emotions? What feelings can you

46

identify? Name one or two. Name a dozen if you know what they are.

Can you explain why you have these feelings?

In a couple of days see if there are any different feelings on your salad bar of emotions.

Laughter at the Funeral

If you have ever been to a funeral, you probably noticed that people acted in various ways. In one corner of the room a person may have been quietly crying. Across the room three or four others may have been telling jokes and laughing. Another group might have been talking about sports or cooking or trips they had taken.

You may even have seen some people doing all three things. They cried one moment, they heard a story and laughed the next, and a few minutes later they were crying again.

The first time you see so much going on, you might be confused. If a funeral is supposed to be sad, why aren't all the people there sad? And why aren't they sad all the time?

Some people who come to the funeral haven't seen each other for a long time. They may be sad about the death but happy to see their friends and relatives. One of the good things about funerals is that they bring people together.

The person who laughs doesn't dislike the person who died. He may have loved her a great deal. His heart may be aching while his face is smiling. Often people at a funeral kid or laugh about something the dead person did. It could be something the dead person used to laugh about, too.

Sadness hurts so badly that we try to push it aside when we can. A person might feel choked up, maybe he can't talk for a few minutes, and then he might talk about a car he bought. People are glad to think about something else. When they are done talking about the car, they might feel the heartache again.

Usually we can't tell how a person feels by how he talks or acts. Many of us hide our feelings inside while we joke around.

Too much joking or kidding could be out of place at a funeral. Too much noise might bother those who are hurting quietly. We all need to respect the feelings of others and not disturb them.

Conversations and friendships have a wholesome place at funerals. Even the right amount of laughter is OK. We simply need to mix it with respect for everyone there.

What Is Cremation?

Have you ever heard of anyone being cremated? The practice of cremation has been popular in England, Japan, India, and Australia, and it is growing in the United States. What does cremation mean, and how is it done?

Basically cremation means that the body will be reduced to ashes by use of extreme heat in something similar to an oven. That heat can either be furnished by fire or electricity.

The process may sound gruesome but it is a quick, efficient way to dispose of a body. We need to remind ourselves that the dead person cannot feel anything and is totally unaware of what is happening. We all know that, but it is important to say it again.

If a relative or friend is going to be cremated and the thought of it bothers you, be sure to discuss it with someone. Explain your questions and fears if you have any. Most of us can adjust to the idea if we get the right information.

Normally no one watches when the body is cremated. Relatives might go to the place where it is done (a crematory or crematorium), but they don't see it take place.

After the body has been reduced to ashes (cremains), these can be given to the family in an urn or a jar. The family then has a number of choices. Some people put the cremains in a vase and keep it on the mantel at home. Some bury the ashes, like they would bury a body, in the ground. Others have the ashes strewn. Strewing means the ashes might be scattered at sea, sprinkled in a forest area, or released from a private airplane.

There are laws to regulate where ashes might be strewn. Some families dispose of the cremains in creative and unusual ways.

Cremation may not be the choice of your family or your religion or your culture. However, it's done frequently today and has been done for thousands of years.

If you have further questions about cremation, be sure to ask your parent or other adults. They may choose to take you to a funeral director, who can tell you more about the subject.

We'll Have New Bodies

Everyone could see how weak Mary's body had become. Her hair was gone, and she had lost almost thirty pounds. One person who visited her in the hospital thought he had walked into the wrong room because he didn't recognize her at first.

Between the cancer and the medicine and the surgery, Mary had dwindled. Her clothes no longer fit, and her skin was loose and wrinkly.

Some illnesses leave our bodies in poor condition. Too often suffering can be seen on our faces and in our eyes.

Among those of us who are Christians there is a strong belief that our old, sick, weak bodies will someday be changed into new bodies. The Bible calls it the resurrection.

Sometime in the future the bodies of those who have died will rise up from the grave or the tomb or the ashes. We will then have new bodies. The Bible doesn't tell us all the details. For instance, will Grandfather have a full head of hair? Will it be brown or gray or what? The Bible promises us a resurrection and new bodies.

Jesus Christ died a terrible death on the cross, and he was buried in a tomb. Three days later he rose up from the dead. That's how we know that a resurrection is possible.

The resurrection of our bodies probably won't happen in three days, but we believe it will happen at God's perfect time. Death is not the final thing that occurs to Christians. Our bodies will rise up again.

"So will it be with the resurrection of the dead. The body that is sown is perishable, it is raised imperishable; it is sown in dishonor, it is raised in glory; it is sown in weakness, it is raised in power; it is sown in a natural body, it is raised a spiritual body" (1 Corinthians 15:42-44).

Uncomfortable Adults

Garrett could see the difference almost immediately. His Aunt Lynn talked about Grandma's death without any difficulty. She described the last hours at the hospital and talked about the funeral arrangements in detail. When Garrett had any questions, Aunt Lynn acted happy to answer them.

But when it came to Garrett's dad, the exact opposite seemed true. He never brought up the subject. If Garrett asked a question, his father would answer it quickly and change the topic to sports or weather or whatever.

Why was Aunt Lynn comfortable with the subject of death while Garrett's father acted like he wanted to run whenever it was mentioned?

Each of us has our own personality. As we grow up and become adults, there are many experiences which contribute to making us who we are. Garrett's father may be uncomfortable with death for several reasons. Let's list a few:

• He might be shy and not talk much anyway.

• Maybe no one has discussed death with him, and he doesn't know how to talk about it.

• He could be afraid of dying himself.

• Maybe he didn't get along with Grandma and now feels guilty, angry, or confused.

• Possibly he is trying to protect Garrett from the subject of death and mistakenly thinks he can keep it from him.

• He might think men are not supposed to cry and is afraid that if he discusses Grandma's death he will lose control.

• There could be another reason which none of us understands and even he does not know.

Wouldn't it be great if all of us could talk about the things that hurt us? Most of us have trouble discussing certain things. Some adults can't talk about money or love or sex or fear. We have blind spots where we can't see clearly, and we may never be able to handle these subjects well.

One way you might be able to help adults is by letting them know that it's all right to talk about death. If they think children don't want to know, then you might tell them that you do want to know.

Make the first move. Ask adults about the hospital, death, the accident, the funeral, or whatever you want. Some adults in your life may be waiting for a child to open them up by asking the right questions.

Thought You Were Over It

Cindy was ten when her grandmother died. No one had known death was coming. At her age of sixty everyone thought Grandmother Rachel would live for many years.

The first couple of weeks Cindy cried a great deal. She and her grandmother had been close and did a lot of things together. Eventually Cindy went on with her life at school, church, and at home. She never forgot her grandmother, but she became busy with activities, responsibilities, and good times.

Almost a month after the funeral Cindy was dusting her dresser and moving things around. As she worked, Cindy picked up a picture of Grandmother Rachel and herself pumping water at a park. Cindy remembered when the picture was taken. They had gone camping upstate together. They had roasted marshmallows and talked "girl stuff," lying on their backs in the tent.

As Cindy dusted the frame, her eyes filled with tears. "Nuts," she whispered to herself as she began to cry. She thought she was over crying by now.

Cindy didn't need to be upset or disappointed. Grief is like that. We grieve because we have lost something. The loss of someone who was important hurts us, and we may never completely get over it.

The day will come when Cindy can dust the picture without crying. But she shouldn't be surprised if once in a while it still makes her sad.

Her grandmother's death and funeral are only a small part of Cindy's memories. They had ten years together. Soon the good memories will begin to flood out the sad ones. She will be able to pick up that same picture and smile as she thinks about the terrific times they had together.

Grief will come back to visit us from time to time. Often we will feel sad when we least expect it. Fortunately the happy thoughts will come back, too. Each is normal, and each is healthy.

When we can choose between the two, it's smarter to emphasize the happy thoughts. They help us cope with grief and help us enjoy life more.

Carlos Buries His Dog

When Carlos's dog, Rowdy, was killed by a car, the boy was shocked and hurt. Rowdy had been the fifth-grader's companion almost every day since their family rescued him from the animal shelter. They had wrestled together on the floor, hiked through the park, and had fun chasing balls. Carlos would toss the old green ball across his backyard, and Rowdy would tear after it full speed and bring it back, his long ears flopping.

Carlos didn't know if he was supposed to cry when his dog was killed, but he did. The tears came naturally, and he didn't try to hold them in.

His father asked Carlos what he wanted to do. Should they together bury the dog, or did Carlos want his father to take care of it? Carlos thought he would like a funeral, and he asked if he could help bury Rowdy.

The two of them dug a deep hole near the wire fence at the back of their yard. Carefully they placed Rowdy's body in the ground and covered it over. Silently, Carlos stood beside the fresh grave and thought his own thoughts. When he was finished, father and son carried their shovels to the garage. That was the way Carlos wanted it, and his father agreed.

Whenever possible, children need to say how they want their dead pets treated. Do we put a dead cat in a simple grave, or do we take it to a pet cemetery? It should be a family decision, and the child needs to express his or her opinion.

Children are like any other people. Some have deep feelings about their pet's death, and others don't care what happens to the body. They may want to flush a dead fish down the toilet, or they might want to bury it. They might want to bury a dead bird, or they might be happy to place it in a box and put it in the trash.

Often children will follow the suggestions of their parents but not always. Adults can't be sure how children feel unless they talk to one another.

Naturally there should be limits. Not many parents will agree to have a pet snake put in a space ship and buried on the moon.

But within reason parent and child certainly can discuss what to do with a dead pet.

Visit the Cemetery?

Our children used to play a game when we drove past a cemetery. The first one to see it would shout, "Cemetery," and instantly all three of them would hold their breath. They acted like something terrible might happen to them if they dared breathe. No one ever explained what awful tragedy would befall them, but they were not taking any chances.

Cemeteries have been known as spooky places. Some people think there might be ghosts or goblins living among the headstones.

It's easy to understand why children are frightened by cemeteries. If they don't know much about death, they might believe stories about strange goings-on around graveyards.

If someone you knew and cared about has died, he may have been placed in a grave at the cemetery. Not everyone is buried, so, if you aren't certain, be sure to ask. How do you feel about going to the gravesite to visit the place where a body is buried?

Some people go to a cemetery *once a year*.

Some people visit a cemetery *more often*.

Some people *never* go to a cemetery.

How does your family feel about visiting a gravesite? Talk it over and find out what everyone is thinking.

What goes on if you visit a cemetery?

Some people stand silently and enjoy their memories.

Some people silently talk to the dead person.

Some people talk out loud to the dead person.

Some people pray.

Some people lay flowers on the grave.

I don't often go to my father's grave, and when I do I don't stay long. My memories are usually pleasant ones. I don't talk to him silently or out loud.

If you go to the cemetery, do what is meaningful to you. You might want to sing a song or read a poem or read Scripture. These are all good things to do.

Not everyone chooses to visit the cemeteries. That's perfectly all right. But you don't need to be afraid to go. Relax and do what you really want to do.

Uncomfortable Words

Some words are harsh. They make people uncomfortable. So we look for gentler ways of saying what we mean.

When a man is out of money, he might say he is "poor" or "broke" or suffers from a "limited cash flow." No matter how he tries to make it sound, he still doesn't have any money.

If a girl is too noisy, you might say she is "hyperactive" or she "needs a nap" or she has "too much energy." But what you really mean is that her screaming is driving you bananas.

We like to make up words or phrases to take the place of the word *dead*. Often we say the person

        has passed away
        has gone to his reward
        is no longer with us
        has expired
        is demised
        is the late Mr. Brown
        has left us
        has cashed in his chips

has joined the angelic choir
is with the angels
has taken his last ride
the Lord took him.

Maybe there are other terms or phrases where you live. Some of them are funny and others are confusing, especially if you haven't heard them before.

In joking, someone might say a person has gone to that "great playground in the sky." There isn't anything wrong with kidding about death if we don't hurt anyone's feelings. But it would be best not to joke with people about the death of their relative.

Whatever word, term, or phrase we use, one thing must be clear as glass—the person is dead.

Dead is dead. A person who has died is gone and will not return. If we use words to soften our conversation, we cannot change the facts. When people die, they are dead. They will never live on earth again.

Who Will Take Care of You?

As we drove from the funeral home toward the cemetery, my son Jim was quiet and still. We had just attended services for a young mother who died in a car accident. She left a husband and two small children behind.

Winding our way past the cemetery gate, we were soon surrounded by headstones and markers.

Finally Jim broke the silence. "If you get killed in a car accident, what will happen to me?"

"Your mother would still be around. She can take care of you," I answered. I was pleased that he had asked.

"What happens," Jim continued, "if she gets killed?"

I began to list the relatives and friends who would come to his aid. Then I asked him who he would like to live with if something like that occurred. To the best of my ability I tried to assure him how unlikely it was that he would lose two parents, but Jim knew it was possible.

Standing by the grave, I felt good about our conversation. Jim needed to know what would happen. Maybe I would have brought it up and maybe not. This way he made sure he had the information he needed to make himself feel secure.

If you want to know, you also should feel free to ask who will take care of you.

Mia Thought about Leaving

"Can I come in?" Mia's mother slowly pushed the bedroom door open.

Mia didn't answer.

"Is this a bad time?" Mother moved toward her daughter.

"Kind of," Mia answered without expression.

"I don't blame you for wanting to be alone." Mother sat on the bed next to her daughter. "It's been tough since Renet has been gone. It's hard on all of us."

Mia didn't speak. Tears filled her eyes without breaking loose onto her cheeks.

"One of these days we need to redecorate this room," Mother continued. "Why don't you start thinking about some different colors."

"I like it this way. It was Renet's favorite color." Mia barely looked around.

"Are you rearranging some of your clothes?"

"Kind of."

"If I didn't know any better, I'd say it looks like you're planning a trip."

Mia didn't answer.

"I hope you aren't planning to leave because of Renet," her mother said. "We all miss her."

"It's hard staying in the same room," Mia sniffled. "Everywhere I look I remember things Renet and I did together. I can't get her out of my mind."

"And you think going away might erase all the memories?" her mother asked.

"I don't know. I guess I need to try something. Sometimes I can't stand it."

"If running away would help, I'd probably run away with you." Her mother took her hand, and Mia didn't pull away. "But if we run away, the loneliness and pain will only get worse.

"Besides, I can't imagine that Renet would have wanted us roaming around the streets like a couple of bag ladies, sleeping in alleys and standing in soup lines. How would that help?"

"What am I going to do?" asked Mia.

"It was bad enough for us to lose one person. We can't afford to lose each other, too. We will always have our good memories of Renet. Let's build more good memories for each other."

"I need to be alone and think," Mia begged.

"I understand. Sometimes I need to be alone, too." Her mother stood to leave. "Just promise me this. You won't leave without telling me good-bye."

"I promise." Mia forced a smile.

Danny's Mean Uncle

Back in the hills of western Pennsylvania lived an eleven-year-old named Danny. A cheerful kid, Danny liked to shoot hoops, ride his skateboard, and play trumpet in the fifth-grade band. He was much like other boys his age except for a little hobby he enjoyed. Danny raised worms in a large rusty bucket out back of his house.

Life trucked along pretty well for this freckle-faced boy until the day that the phone call came. His mother took the call. Her brother Roger, Danny's uncle, had died suddenly of a heart attack. The shock was terrible. Danny's mother cried all night. Friends and relatives rushed over to see her, and many of them cried, too.

Soon the funeral arrangements were set. More people came to the house. More people cried.

Danny, the normally cheerful boy, wanted to cry. He tried to cry. But somehow Danny couldn't quite force the tears.

"The fact is," he thought to himself, "it's a big relief to have Uncle Roger gone."

Uncle Roger had always treated him mean. Danny hated to see him come over to the house. Every visit meant more pain and embarrassment for Danny.

Uncle Roger would twist Danny's arms and wrists until they hurt. He would make fun of the boy's clothes and pick on his friends if they were around. Then Uncle Roger would argue mercilessly. It was as if he liked to start verbal fights with his nephew. Past the point of simple teasing, Roger would jump on a subject and put Danny down over and over again.

A good kid, Danny didn't like to complain. It seemed so strange that he actually disliked his own uncle. But the fact was he hated to see him show up.

And now Uncle Roger was dead. He left a wife and two children. Most people were crying. Danny wasn't.

Not that Danny was glad that his uncle had died. *Glad* wouldn't exactly describe it. But Danny was relieved to have him gone. He wouldn't have to take all of that pain anymore.

It's Final

Death was terribly confusing to me when I was a little kid. I would go to the movies and see people get shot. Those deaths looked real to me. After a while I decided that they were using criminals for actors and shooting them while they made the movie. As you can tell, I was very young.

I don't know how long I held onto this idea, but soon I noticed problems with it. Some people who were killed in a particular movie were then killed again in another movie six months later.

There went my whole attempt to understand death in the movies.

I can imagine that when you were younger you also tried to understand death on television and in the movies. I wouldn't be surprised if you had an explanation of death every bit as odd as mine.

On the screen death doesn't seem to be forever. People die from cancer this week, and they show up on another series a month later. A viewer can get the idea that death is only for a short time.

Just as confusing are the movies about relatives coming back as ghosts. The stories are fun and often funny, but they aren't real. Uncle Ted isn't going to come back later and live in your basement. Cousin Lulu isn't going to return from the dead and try to fix up dates at the local high school for your big sister.

Death is final!

We may go later to join our deceased relatives in heaven. The Bible gives us that hope to look forward to. But Aunt Zelda isn't going to come back and talk to us at the car wash.

Just thought we should get that straight.

Unusual Deaths

Some deaths are hard to talk about because they are unusual. They may even be embarrassing to us. Because of the amount of ignorance and prejudice held by many people, some of us feel ashamed when a relative dies for one of those reasons. But we don't need to feel odd.

Two of the causes of death which make people the most uncomfortable are AIDS and suicide. Many of us whisper about such deaths. We are afraid our friends won't understand and might think we are strange.

The good news is that more of us are becoming educated about each of those problems.

Recently a teenager in our part of the state died from AIDS. He received the virus from a blood transfusion when he was a child. Not only was he brave, but the young man also wanted to be helpful. He spent a lot of his time trying to educate other young people about the disease. Hundreds of people attended his funeral.

I have met families who have lost relatives to AIDS. They have been terrific people who deserve our care and understanding.

As the public learns more about this disease, hopefully we will become more loving toward the victims and their families. If we have a relative who has AIDS, we may need special friends to talk to. Counselors, youth workers, teachers, and ministers are often good listeners and may have some suggestions that could help.

We know that some people won't understand, so we simply stay clear of them. But there are many others who will prove to be excellent friends.

The same problems are faced by the families of those who end their own life. It's hard to talk about the suicide of a relative or a friend. We have enough trouble understanding what happened, and we can't expect others to understand it either.

Suicide is often called the death they "whisper about" because friends simply don't know what to say. Look for those special people who are accepting and kind. If a suicide has touched our lives, we need to discuss it with someone.

The families I have known who have suffered from a relative's suicide have usually been nice, normal people. But some people don't realize that, and they tend to avoid families like this. Others, because of ignorance, think there is something wrong with a family whose relative has committed suicide.

Fortunately most people don't react as badly to either of those deaths as they used to. There is hope. We may not be able to discuss suicide and AIDS with everyone, but we can talk about them with someone.

Shoulds and Oughts

"You shouldn't be out playing. Your aunt's funeral is this afternoon."

How much sense does that make? Maybe playing is one of the best things you can do. Playing doesn't mean you didn't like your aunt. Good activities might be a great way for you to deal with how you feel.

People mean well when they tell us what we should do, but shoulds aren't always the best.

"I think you ought to stay home from school an extra day. There's no sense in going back too early."

Whoever said that wanted to protect you. But who can say which way will help the most? Maybe getting back with your friends at school will be a big help. In many cases you have a good sense of when you need to return to school.

Instead of using oughts, we can discuss what seems best for the situation.

"There will be visitors coming to the

funeral home on Monday and Tuesday nights. You really should be there to greet the people."

How do you feel? Are two nights too many? Would you prefer thirty minutes each evening? Is there some way to compromise so that most of the people involved will be satisfied with the arrangement?

You are "people" too, and sometimes you need to be included in the decision making. Sometimes you may have to go along with plans made by others, but when possible you should be there when the plans are made.

Too many shoulds and oughts without asking you get out of hand.

"You ought to be a pallbearer. You don't want people to think that you didn't like your uncle, do you?"

This is a heavy *ought*. But what if you would rather not? Maybe you are sad and don't want to participate. Maybe the thought of being a pallbearer scares you. Maybe you didn't like your uncle and something was seriously wrong between the two of you. Maybe you just want to stand back. And probably you don't want to explain it right now.

Be polite. Be direct. Don't let the "ought" people dump more on you than you can take.

Trouble Sleeping

After his grandfather died, Cody noticed that his life was changing. Cody worried a lot. He wasn't always sure what he was worrying about, but things often bothered him. The young boy missed his grandfather and thought about him daily.

Cody wasn't exactly nervous. He used to act pretty cool, and nothing rattled him much. But now it was different. Grumpy, edgy, uptight—those words would describe Cody well.

The worst times were at night. In the dark he could picture his grandfather lying in the coffin. He didn't like that sight, so he tried to remember Grandfather playing in the yard or out camping in a park.

Cody couldn't sleep as well as he used to. A couple of times he wet the bed. That was embarrassing and hard to explain. He wasn't sure if he failed to wake up or if he woke up and was afraid to get up or exactly why it did happen.

Everybody told Cody to act like a big boy, so he didn't want to admit that he had a problem. He hoped that in a day or two it would all go away. But it didn't.

After four or five days of feeling miserable, Cody finally went to his mother and told her what was going on. She wasn't surprised. She had noticed that he wasn't eating right and that half of the time he was spaced out at the supper table.

Cody's mother explained that she had some of the same feelings. She still pictured Grandfather in the coffin. On the one hand it was a rough memory, but on the other hand Grandfather looked like he was at peace. She liked that, especially since he had looked so miserable in the hospital.

She noticed that she was more jittery than normal, too. "That's what happens when you lose someone important to you," she told him. "For a while you feel unsettled and uncertain, and you wonder how you are going to adjust."

After a couple of talks with his mother, Cody began to relax. Soon he slept the whole night through. He has never forgotten his grandfather, and he never will. But Cody thinks about the good memories, and he feels good about them.

The death of Cody's grandfather shook him up like what happens when you shake up a two-liter bottle of cola. Inside he felt like things were bubbling and fizzing and erupting. Sometimes he thought he might blow up.

A simple conversation with his mother was like loosening the top on that bottle. Some of the fizz came out, and pressure was released. Less pressure made Cody feel like a new person.

True or False?

Most of us are uncomfortable discussing death. When it happens, we aren't sure what to say and frequently we say the wrong things. The following is a list of things that people often say. Read each statement and answer true or false. The correct answer follows each question. First the statement and then the right reply.

God needed more choir members in heaven, so he took Mrs. Parker because she has a beautiful voice.
If God is making up heavenly choirs, he already has millions of good voices to choose from. God doesn't go around breaking up families simply to find a soprano for a mixed quartet.

Grandpa's heart stopped beating while he was asleep last night, and he went to heaven without waking up.
This could be exactly what happened. He didn't die because he was sleeping, but he may have died while he was sleeping. God

welcomed him into heaven when he arrived.

Our little sister died, and now she is an angel in heaven.
If we choose to believe this we can, but the fact is angels are angels and people are people. God wouldn't take a person if he wanted an angel. That would be like the zoo running short of monkeys, so they go out to buy cats.

It sounds good to say that people become angels. Don't argue with anyone who thinks they do. But remember that horses don't die and become eagles.

Remember, only the good die young.
Whoever made this one up meant well, too, but think it through for a minute. That statement means that all of the old people must be bad because they have lived so long. Death has nothing to do with being good or bad.

Your mother has died and gone to heaven. She lives there with Jesus, and she will be there when you arrive a long time from now.

Sounds great. This may well be the case. Christians have always believed that those who trust Jesus go to heaven when they die.

Grandfather has died, but he will be in heaven keeping an eye on you. Be sure you don't mess up.

According to this, Grandfather has become that great moral police officer in the sky. If we believed this, instead of picturing a loving relative, we would live in daily fear of some spiritual detective who is peeping through our keyhole. There is no reason to accept this one.

The person who said it is trying to control our behavior and is using a dead man to do it. There are a lot of reasons to behave well, but this isn't one of them.

The best things we can say about death are always truthful. None of us should make up ghost stories or beautiful scenes to try to explain death. If we are talking about faith and what we hope is happening, we should say so. There is nothing wrong with speaking about God or heaven or hope, but we should be careful that what we say is as accurate as possible.

Nobody Knows Exactly

If your grandfather dies, no one knows exactly how you feel. I might say, "My grandfather died, too, and I know just how you feel." But that wouldn't be entirely true.

Whatever your grandfather meant to you would be different from what my grandfather meant to me. Maybe you were very close to him or maybe you hardly knew your grandfather. Some of us have a grandfather living next door. Others have a grandfather living in Australia. Every relationship is different, and everyone has his or her own feelings.

A few people have relatives who are actually mean. Those people won't miss their relatives at all when they die. Each of us has our own way of feeling.

People say, "I know how you feel" because they want to be helpful. They actually don't know until you tell them how you feel, and even then they don't totally understand.

If your father would die, you might feel a dozen different ways. When my father died, I felt bad, confused, relieved, happy for him, and a bucketful of other emotions. Other people have their own feelings when their fathers die. Some feelings will be the same as mine were, but others will be just the opposite.

When people say, "I know exactly how you feel," that statement has a way of shutting us down. If they think they know all about our emotions, what's the point in trying to explain them? That's not the best way to start a conversation.

There is only one way to know exactly how you feel. You can tell someone and explain your emotions. Otherwise everyone is simply guessing. You can discuss your sense of loss, your pain, your fear, your contentment, your faith, or anything you want.

There are no "good" emotions or "bad" emotions. Emotions are how you really feel. If you are angry, it's all right to be angry. Explain to someone why you are angry. There's nothing wrong with feeling numb. Can you tell someone why you feel numb?

When a friend says she knows exactly how you feel, you might reply, "Would you

89

like to hear how I feel?" She will probably say yes, and you will be able to talk to her.

Don't let her shut you down because she said the wrong thing. Pick up on the conversation and start discussing how you really do feel.

Megan's Missing Doll

When Megan was a little girl she often played with her toys in the yard. She had two or three dolls, an old beat-up dollhouse, and a tin kitchen set complete with pots and pans. She felt happy and carefree playing in the open air on sunny afternoons.

One day while she was playing, Megan remembered a red wagon she liked and went inside the house to get it. In a few minutes Megan returned with her wagon. Almost immediately she sensed that something was wrong.

Megan looked around carefully. She looked at the dollhouse, the kitchen set, and her pots and pans. Then she checked her dolls. Tara was there. Dawn was there. Kristi was . . . Where was Kristi?

Jumping to her feet, Megan looked all around the yard for her missing doll. After searching behind every bush and tree, she ran frantically into the house.

Even though Megan and her family combed the backyard, they could not find

Kristi. The doll was gone and was never seen again.

For the next couple of days Megan stayed away from her backyard. She didn't feel comfortable there. Then slowly, a few at a time, Megan began to bring her dolls and house and pots and pans outside again. But now she never left her stuff in the yard. If Megan went inside, even for a few minutes, she carried her dolls with her.

After we lose something important, we begin to worry that maybe we might lose another important thing, too.

If we lose a parent, a grandparent, a brother or a sister in death, we wonder if we will lose someone else. Death makes us worry. It makes us realize how easily people can slip away.

Almost anything can happen. We've all been around long enough to know that. No one can promise us that death will not come to a person we love. All we can say is that it almost never happens right away. We've heard stories of relatives who have died one week or one month or one year after each other. But those situations are rare.

Time usually helps. A month or two months after a death we worry less about another relative dying. It's all right to be afraid at first, but with time the fear should become less and less.

Megan became more careful and loving toward the dolls she still had. She also learned to enjoy being with them and playing together again.

Getting in Touch

Have you ever come home after playing all day and sat on the couch next to your mother or father? You were tired, worn out, hungry and a little sleepy. While you sat there talking for a few minutes, did you rest your head on your parent's shoulder? Did you feel better because there was a warm, friendly arm to lean on?

When someone we care about dies, our feeling of loss wears us out. Our heart aches, our lips may tremble, and our tears may run like a stream. We grow tired of thinking. We try to understand death, and we try to figure out what will happen next. We may not get enough sleep and may not eat enough. In a word, we're exhausted.

In a time like this you might feel better if you could touch a close and caring relative. There is something about touching that gives added strength. You might not feel so frazzled if someone would hold you or hug you.

Naturally you don't hold and hug everybody. Do you have people—a parent, an aunt, or even a cousin—whom you feel particularly close to? Why not sit next to them or put your arm around them or hold their hands? Touching has the power to calm us down and soothe us.

When there are deaths and funerals, often there is a great deal of talking. Talking might be a big help. But healthy holding is important, too. Holding makes us feel wanted, cared for, and loved. Holding means we are close to someone, and we are not alone.

Usually there is a lot of holding and hugging when a person dies. Those who are left behind feel like they need each other. But if your relatives seem too shy to hold each other, you might need to take the first step. Take someone's hand if you want to. Kiss a relative on the cheek if you would like to. Wrap an arm around his or her shoulder.

Snuggling can help too. Snuggle up against someone in a chair or on a couch. Just letting your arms or legs touch might mean as much as a giant hug.

Not only do *you* need to be held, but your family members need it, too. Be helpful. Give your Aunt Lacey a tight squeeze.

Toss your arm around Uncle Mark's waist. They will probably scrunch you back and you'll both feel better.

Jesus' disciples were surprised when he took the children up into his arms. But he did it anyway. The children must have appreciated the hug, and Jesus did, too.

"And he took the children in his arms, put his hands on them and blessed them" (Mark 10:16).

Too Old to Cry?

When are we too old to cry?

Grandparents, police officers, football coaches, teachers, and cheerleaders all know how to cry. They aren't too old or too big or too brave. When their hearts hurt or they have lost someone important to them, they might cry.

I knew a minister who preached a sermon at a funeral, and when he finished speaking, he cried. He wasn't too old or too adult. He did what he felt like doing.

Are twelve-year-olds too old to cry?

Not if they want to. Many eleven- or twelve-year-olds fight hard to hold back their tears, but there isn't anything wrong with crying. Some children try to keep from crying because they think crying is for little kids. But crying is for everyone who feels the need to do it.

Is it all right for boys to cry?

Some people discourage boys from crying. Some adults say, "Now be a big boy and don't cry." When boys hear that, they struggle to keep all of their tears inside. They feel embarrassed if even one lonely tear escapes and runs down their cheek.

Big boys and young men should be permitted to cry just like anyone else.

What if you don't feel like crying?

Then don't. None of us has to cry. There are no rules that say now it's time to cry. Later you might cry when you least expect to. Maybe you will never cry about this death. That's OK, too.

Some people feel terrible about the death of a parent or friend and yet they don't cry. If adults don't cry, don't think they don't care. They might be crying inside. They might ache and hurt. Their throat might be tight with sadness and still they don't cry.

One of the best things you can do is not to pretend. If the tears flow, let them flow. If the tears don't come, don't try to make them. Be as natural as you can.

Two thousand years ago Jesus Christ attended the funeral of a friend named Lazarus. He saw the members of Lazarus's family crying, and soon Jesus was crying, too.

There is nothing wrong with crying when it comes from our true feelings. "Jesus wept" (John 11:35).

Will I Die, Too?

All of us think about it. We don't usually think about it every day, but we all wonder sometimes. If other people die, that must mean that we are going to die sometime, too.

You probably don't worry about it too much when you see an old person die, but sometimes you hear about a child who has died. The child may have been only nine or twelve years old, and he or she isn't alive anymore.

It makes you think.

Let's look at the facts. Life is fragile, but it is also tough. People could die easily, but most of us don't. We may get sick, we may get in an accident, but most of us live for a long time. Some of us live for seventy or eighty years or even longer.

Once in a while a child dies. When that happens, it's doubly sad. But it doesn't happen to most of us. Some children have to live in wheelchairs, but that doesn't happen to most of us. Some children are blind, but that doesn't happen to most of us.

There are no guarantees. No one can promise you that you will live to be a grandparent, but most people around us do live that long.

You've thought about death. That's good to think about it. We should all remember that we won't live on this earth forever. The best thing we can do now is to spend most of our time thinking about life. Life is where we are now. We should enjoy life. We should love those around us. We should help others. And we should serve God. It would be a shame to waste today by worrying about tomorrow.

Jesus taught us to concentrate on today. We have plenty to handle. There is schoolwork to do, there are games to play, models to build, trips to take, rooms to clean, shows to watch, friends to help, pizzas to eat, skits to do, and even cars to wash. Don't sit around waiting to die. There are too many exciting things to get involved in today.

"Therefore do not worry about tomorrow, for tomorrow will worry about itself. Each day has enough trouble of its own" (Matthew 6:34).

Is Death Punishment?

Did you ever hear someone say that if we are bad God might get angry and cause us to die? That person pictures God as a giant grump in the sky walking around zapping people who get out of line.

Does God punish us by taking life away? It's a good question. Millions ask that sometime. If a dad or an aunt or a brother dies, does that prove that God is upset?

To find the answer let's look at two places for information. Let's look at the people around us, and then let's look at the Bible.

The newspapers and television tell us almost daily about people who do terrible things. They murder, they steal, and commit loads of miserable acts toward others. If they get caught, these same people go to prison for twenty to thirty years.

It's obvious that God doesn't cause these people to die. They do evil things, and yet God allows them to live.

Since that's true, it's hard to believe that God caused our Aunt Hilda from Milwaukee to die because she gossiped. It's difficult to think that a brother died because he stole baseball cards.

The evidence doesn't make sense. God isn't in the business of ending lives when people mess up.

Second, let's look at the Bible to see what it tells us about God and how he operates.

First, David wrote a psalm that says *God's love is always with us.*

"For your love is ever before me, and I walk continually in your truth" (Psalm 26:3).

Second, *God loves us even when we mess up.*

"But God demonstrates his own love for us in this: While we were still sinners, Christ died for us" (Romans 5:8).

Third, *God wants to do what is good for each of us.* He isn't interested in hurting us.

"You are forgiving and good, O Lord, abounding in love to all who call to you" (Psalm 86:5).

When someone we love dies, it must make God sad for us. He is sad to see us separated from each other. At the same time God is happy to have members of his family come and live with him.

God isn't looking for ways to hurt us. Rather he is interested in ways to help.

Juan's Wish Didn't Come True

Juan had a little sister. Her name was Jolanda. Jolanda was part girl and part wrecking machine. What Juan's four-year-old sister seemed to enjoy the most was messing up her brother's room.

When Juan was at school, Jolanda would sneak into his room and get into everything. She would push the keys on his video game, put his tapes out of order, and run his cars all over the floor.

Nearly every day after school Juan would come home, look at his bedroom, and get terribly angry. One look at his floor and Juan would run after Jolanda and yell at her at the top of his lungs. But nothing seemed to help. His mother would talk to Jolanda, but the wrecking machine kept up its destructive work.

One day was worse than any other. Juan opened the door to his room and saw his favorite model, the battleship *U.S.S. Missouri*, smashed on the floor. Juan had it nearly half finished and it had taken a long time. Always after he worked on his prized model, he would carefully place it on the top shelf in his room so Jolanda couldn't get to it.

But that day Jolanda had climbed up, and the battleship fell to the floor, breaking into dozens of pieces. Juan was furious.

"I wish she was dead!" Juan blurted out. Sometimes brothers and sisters say that when they are tremendously upset.

Juan put his battleship back together again and forgot what he had said. Nearly a month later Jolanda dashed into the street while chasing a ball, and a car hit her. Three hours later Jolanda died in the hospital.

Juan felt awful. It was bad enough to lose his sister in death, but Juan was sure he had caused her to die.

All of us say terrible things sometimes. We may think we mean them when we say them, but the situation calms down and life goes on.

There is no way that Juan could have caused Jolanda's death. Making a wish has *never* caused anyone to die. People die when their bodies stop working.

Someone should tell Juan that it wasn't his fault.

How Can You Help?

When one grandparent dies, everyone feels sorry for the other grandparent. The surviving grandparent loved that person, and now life may be terribly lonely and hard. At first many relatives and friends come around and try to help in any way they can. They may bring food or clean the house or sit and talk.

Often children feel sorry for the grandparent who is alone, and they would like to help, too. That's a great idea. Children can take out the trash, look at old pictures with the grandparent, go to the store, or run errands.

There is plenty that you can do as a child, but you can't do it all. Some children will try to make it their job to cheer up a relative or friend who is hurting. They think that if they do enough things they could make that person happy again.

These children mean well, but they can't necessarily make a person happy again. You should never feel like it is your job to make someone get over grief. You can help—a little—but you can't do it all by yourself.

If you live far away, you can make phone calls or write letters. Once or twice you might even send a present. You could make an audio- or videotape and send it. These aren't things you have to do, but each of them can be helpful.

You should never feel like you are responsible for making anyone happy again. That's too heavy a burden.

Be nice and thoughtful. Children often have a special ability to touch someone's life. That's why many adults like to have children around at the time of a death.

Take their hands. Give them hugs. Tell them you love them if you choose. But never make the whole job yours.

Don't Be Superstitious

When Trudy handed the change to her mother, her mom gasped with shock.

"Take this two-dollar bill outside and burn it right away. Do it now," she demanded. "There are matches on the kitchen table."

Bewildered, Trudy accepted the two-dollar bill and started for the kitchen.

"Two-dollar bills are bad luck," her mother continued. "If there is one in the house, a death will soon follow."

Even though we are smart and educated, some of us still manage to believe in superstitions. Believing a superstition means we believe that if we do some things, good or bad will come from our actions. Some baseball players are afraid to step on a white line because they think it's bad luck. Other players won't shave if their team is on a winning streak. Some girls won't step on a crack in the sidewalk. I even heard of a surgeon who didn't like to operate without his "lucky" shoes.

Have you ever seen a person say something good and then knock on wood?

Someone might say, "Well, actually my business is going well, knock on wood." Some people are afraid that when they brag, bad luck will soon come if they don't knock on wood. That's a superstition.

When I was a child, one of my parents would fuss immediately if I started to open an umbrella in the house. Many people believed that an open umbrella in the house would cause someone to die.

Some people still think that walking under a ladder, breaking a mirror, or a black cat crossing your path means something terrible will happen. Those things sound silly, but many of us still believe strange things.

In some areas of the country people are afraid when they hear thunder on a sunny day. That is supposed to mean that someone will die.

Superstitions might be harmless fun, but they also can be dangerous. Imagine if someone left the top off the milk jug and a relative should happen to die the next day. Wouldn't it be terrible if the person who left the top off thought he caused that person to die?

All of us need to know that superstitions aren't true. We don't cause "lucky" and "unlucky" things to happen. If we carry a rabbit's foot, our day doesn't really go better because we have a furry paw with us.

The sad thing is that some children believe that they did something that caused a relative to die. If you think that, you need to talk to someone you trust. You should explain what you believe you have done. A smart adult can help you understand that it isn't true.

Superstitions don't cause people to die.

Cobwebs in Your Hair

"Mandie said she invited you to the skating party Friday, but you didn't want to go," Jana's mother said. She was stacking plates in the dishwasher after her daughter scraped them.

"No, I just don't feel like it," Jana mumbled.

"You can't stay in the house forever, you know." Her mother pushed the glasses into place.

"I know that but . . ."

"Isn't it time to start calling your friends again?" Mother closed the drawer and turned on the machine.

"Oh, sure, that sounds easy," Jana raised her voice. "How can you even think about going places when Grandma just died? I don't understand you."

"I do understand." Mother tossed her cloth on the sink. "Grandma's death hurts me as much as it does you. But I'm not going to lock myself in the basement and cover my head with a sack."

Jana's voice rose another level. "So, what am I supposed to do—go out and

party and just forget about my own grandmother?"

"That isn't what I'm going to do." Jan-
a's mother moved closer and gently hugged
her young daughter. "I'll never forget your
grandmother. I've got too many good
memories for that. But I don't think that
she would be happy if she knew I was
sitting in the corner letting cobwebs form
in my hair."

"It doesn't seem right to just snap out
of it," Jana objected.

"I don't know how it seems." Her
mother wiped a tear from her daughter's
cheek. "But I do know that she would want
me to enjoy myself." She squeezed her
daughter. "Besides, you wouldn't look all
that good with cobwebs in your hair."

You're Not an Adult

Do some adults still say things like this: "Now that your father has died, you know you have to be the man of the house around here" or "With the death of your mother, you have to step in and take care of the children now"?

People who say those things mean well, but they have said too much. Children can't become adults when a parent dies.

We've all heard of families who lost both parents in death, and a teenager took over to raise the children. But this seldom happens. In almost every case other caring adults will come to take charge of the family.

There are ways each member of the family can help. Each person may have to pitch in and take a few extra jobs around the house. But no child should try to become an adult.

Take your time and grow up one stage at a time. If you miss out on being a child now, it's too hard to go back and become a child when you are thirty years old.

If Aunt Lydia puts her arm around you and says, "You're going to be the mom now," smile back if you want. But say to yourself, "No, I'm not. I'm too busy being myself."

A Day to Keep Busy

Every year on March 14, Melissa gets together with some friends. They don't exactly have a party, but they do plan an activity. Three or four of them either go out to eat or go bowling. One year they went roller skating and skated until their feet got sore.

March 14 is an important day to Melissa because that was the day her brother Tony was killed in a car accident. Every year she remembers that terrible day, and Melissa knows she needs to keep busy.

She doesn't plan a party to celebrate on that day. But the eleven-year-old does arrange an activity and collects some friends because she doesn't like to be alone on the day she will never forget.

Melissa still thinks about Tony's death. Last year she also visited the cemetery with her mother on that day. She remembers, but she refuses to brood over it. Sometimes Melissa even smiles when she thinks about how happy Tony must be in heaven. But no matter how positive she tries to be, the separation still hurts. Melissa misses her older brother and wishes they could spend some time together.

When we lose someone as important as a brother or a sister, we usually grieve for a long time. For most of us the grief never goes away entirely. But smart people try to soften the grief by staying busy with friends and relatives.

Nothing will ever replace what we have lost, but Melissa refuses to let her loss run her life.

Be Active

It's easy to sit around when you're sad. People sit in the house, sit at the funeral home, sit in the car, and sit on the floor. We may be sitting or lying around on couches and on beds.

No one feels like doing much. But sitting around wears us out.

Maybe we need to make extra effort to force ourselves to become a little active. Take a walk for a few minutes. Jog around the block. Do a dozen sit-ups. Go out and shoot some hoops.

Too much inactivity can make our problems worse. Moving loosens up our bodies, wakes up our brains, and improves our spirits.

Don't be too noisy if some members of the family want to be quiet. Look for some silent ways to put your muscles in motion.

None of us can say what the deceased person would think about children playing. We can't ask them. But my guess is that most of our friends and relatives who have died would have been happy to see the children doing something. If those who have died could still be here, they might want to be active with us.

Activity doesn't have to be disrespectful. If we play catch, we aren't going to forget the person who died.

When the time seems right, look for a ball or ask if you can go for a walk. Activity helps clean the cobwebs out of our brains.

The Next Life Is Better

Which do you enjoy the most—playing video games or ice skating? Where is your favorite place to go—to the local shopping mall or to a state park? Which food would you choose first—a banana split or pizza with gobs of cheese and hamburger? Who are some of your best friends—people at school or someone in your neighborhood?

When we don't feel grumpy, we have to admit there are plenty of things to enjoy in this life. We like to go places, do things and play with our pets.

But someday we will each have to leave this world when we die. And this life seems so good for most of us that we would hate to leave it.

Fortunately leaving this life through death isn't as terrible as we might think.

I remember standing by the hospital bed of an old man who was dying. He had enjoyed living. He loved his family, and they loved him. His heart had become very weak and couldn't keep working much longer.

As we talked, I asked him how he felt about dying. The old man smiled and told me how much he looked forward to it. He said he wanted to leave this life and go to be with God.

Some people are afraid to die, but many others think of death as a trip into the presence of God. Once there, they will never die again but live forever with our heavenly Father.

One of the writers of the Bible thought of death as being better than this life. He wrote: "A good name is better than fine perfume, and the day of death better than the day of birth" (Ecclesiastes 7:1).

When people die, we may miss them, but we don't have to feel sorry for them. They go to be part of the family of God in heaven because they belong to Jesus Christ.

Jesus and the Welcoming Committee

The picnic didn't begin until ten o'clock, but Sara and Matt went early. They picked out an area at the park and pulled three or four tables together. Matt tied a sign to a telephone pole. The sign said AN-DERSON PICNIC and had a red arrow at the bottom pointing to the site. Meanwhile, Sara found two trees the right distance apart and began to untangle the volleyball net.

This was something the two of them enjoyed. They liked to prepare the area so the cousins and aunts and uncles would know where to go when they arrived. Matt and Sara wanted everyone to enjoy the picnic as much as they did.

The Bible tells us that 2,000 years ago Jesus Christ left this earth to go and prepare a place for us. We don't know exactly where it is or what it looks like, so let's say it is a "heavenly picnic." We do know that Jesus has put everything in order, and he will head up the welcoming committee when we get there.

Sooner or later all of us will leave this earth. Our bodies may be placed in the ground or cremated, but something about us will leave. We could call it our soul or our spirit or our personality. Let's think of it as the real us. The real us escapes from our weak or broken bodies and takes off for the "heavenly picnic."

When we get there, Jesus will have picked out a spot for us, pulled the tables together, and even gotten a cabin ready for us. That's all important because we are going to stay there a long time.

Can you picture Jesus on the picnic grounds, his arms wide open, welcoming us as we arrive? The Bible tells us it will all happen something like that.

Jesus is the one we can trust in this life, and we can also count on him in the next life. Eventually we will break out of this world and head for the "Great Picnic." Jesus said,

"I am going there to prepare a place for you" (John 14:2).

We're Never Alone

When death comes close to us, it's a deep sadness. The pain and loss are real, and it takes us some time to learn how to deal with the separation.

Fortunately there is hope for all of us because we are never alone. We have a heavenly Father who stays by our side no matter what problems we face. God gives us the courage, the strength, the peace, and the reason to go on with our lives.

God promises to be with us on both the good days and the tough ones.

We, like David, can be confident that the Lord is with us no matter how tough the circumstances.

"Even though I walk through the valley of the shadow of death, I will fear no evil, for you are with me; your rod and your staff, they comfort me" (Psalm 23:4).